Spices of the World

Jill Norman

The International Wine & Food Society

This Monograph – the twentieth in the series – is
published in 2019 by
The International Wine & Food Society Ltd,
under the chairmanship of Andrew Jones.

ISBN 978-0-900813-04-7

Text © Jill Norman 2019

The International Wine & Food Society Ltd
4 St James's Square, London SW1Y 4JU, UK
www.iwfs.org +44(0)20 7827 5732

Acknowledgements
I am grateful to Rajiv Kehr and to Rajan Karunakaran for sharing their
thoughts on matching drinks to spicy foods.

Edited by Katie Wyartt
Designed by Jayne Clementson
Printed in the UK by All Things Print, CO6 1RY

Contents

Introduction	2
1. Using spices at home	5
2. The history of spices	9
3. An A-Z of spices	15
4. Spice mixtures	59
5. Matching spicy food and wine	63
Where to buy spices	69
Bibliography	70

Introduction

What are spices, where do they come from and how are they usually characterised?

The Oxford English Dictionary defines spices as "one or other of various strongly flavoured or aromatic substances of vegetable origin, obtained from tropical plants, commonly used in condiments". Most spices are derived from tropical plants – from the roots, bark, seeds, buds and fruits, and are usually used in dried form, whether whole or ground.

Most of the important spice plants – cinnamon, cardamom, cloves, ginger, nutmeg and pepper – are native to tropical Asia, while allspice, chillies and vanilla come from the Americas. Many aromatic seeds, such as coriander, fenugreek, fennel and mustard, are from the Mediterranean basin, and Europe's colder regions have contributed caraway, dill and juniper.

Complex aromas
Spices differ from herbs, which are usually green, fresh, aromatic plants that grow in relatively mild climates and are consumed fresh or dried. Some, such as garlic and horseradish, have similar strong flavours to those found in spices. Broadly speaking, herbs are the basis of much flavouring of European food, whereas almost all spices come from areas with hotter climates and therefore tend to feature prominently in cuisine from these regions.

> **The oleoresins contain the aroma profile of the plant, and provide the spice's characteristic flavour**

INTRODUCTION

Our first impression of any food or drink comes through our eyes, then we smell the sometimes complex aromas and, finally, we taste. Four specific tastes can be detected in different parts of the mouth – sweet, sour, salty and bitter – and pungency can be detected in taste, too.

We smell spices as soon as we open the packaging, and later as the aromas develop in cooking. Tasting a dry spice, with few exceptions, is not rewarding, however we can appreciate their flavours in a cooked dish.

Characterising spices

The characteristic odour of spices derives from the volatile constituents in the plant material. The oleoresins, which can be drawn out by carbon dioxide extraction, contain the aroma profile of the plant. They provide the spice's characteristic flavour, but the pungent principle – the hot sensation produced in the mouth by spices such as chillies, pepper or ginger – also contributes to flavour.

Our vocabulary for describing smell and taste is fairly limited; often they are described in terms of other aromas and flavours. When we are discussing spices, "aromatic" and "pungent" are commonly used words, but they don't offer an accurate definition.

One group of spices could be defined as warm and earthy: saffron, cardamom, cumin, caraway and turmeric, for example. Within the group there are other aromas and flavours to detect. Saffron is musky, floral and penetrating; cardamom mellow and fruity, slightly camphorous; cumin spicy-sweet with a bitter note; and caraway bittersweet with a hint of anise. Turmeric, when fresh, has gingery, citrus aromas, but the dried version is citrus, musky and slightly bitter. Of course, different people have different perceptions when it comes to aromas and flavours.

Scientific developments

Today, food scientists use e-noses and e-tongues to make sensory evaluations of foods because they are more consistent than human noses and tongues. They collect headspace – aroma molecules, gathered from a range of spices, herbs and other foods, are reproduced in laboratories for use in ready-prepared foods. Flavour drops, originally developed for the NASA space food programme, are now available online in an extensive range of foods, including many spices. Concentrated natural spice and herb pastes are available, too. If you want to experiment, proceed cautiously – only one drop, heavily diluted, may be needed. The flavour profile of many of these drops and pastes is impressive, but many nutritive, tactile and cultural values are lost.

1. Using spices at home

Understanding how best to store spices at home, and how to use them in cooking, can be complex

Always use spices sparingly, either alone or combined with other spices or herbs. It is best to buy whole spices and then grind them as needed. All spices lose their oleoresins and volatile oils over time, and whole spices hold them for longer than ground.

All dry spices should be stored in a cupboard rather than on an open shelf. The best packaging for spices is small resealable foil pouches – when tightly closed they protect the contents from light and humidity.

Small airtight tins or dark glass or plastic pots are the next best containers, but even those with airtight lids have a space above the contents that allows air to enter.

Crush or grind

Use a spice or coffee grinder (but don't also grind coffee in it) and grind to a powder as needed. Some spices need only to be crushed, and for this a pestle and mortar is best. Or, for a large amount, put the spices in a plastic bag, flatten it on a worktop and crush with a rolling pin. As before, don't crush more than you need.

A few spices, such as dried galangal, are almost impossible to grind at home, so buy ground. Fresh ginger and galangal are best grated, while dry ginger and turmeric are very hard and are best grated on a rasp or a fine citrus grater. The Japanese use an oroshigane grater for wasabi.

> **It is best to buy whole spices and then grind them as needed**

If you have spices that have been on the shelf for several months or longer, it is worth checking to see if they have retained their aromatic profile. Try breaking a piece of cinnamon, grinding a few seeds or crushing a cardamom pod – if you can't smell the aroma then throw them away. Some ground spices can lose their aromatic qualities over the course of a few months.

Lemongrass, curry leaves and makrut lime leaves can be frozen in plastic boxes or tightly sealed bags and will keep for several months. Once thawed, use immediately.

Cooking with spices
Spices are frequently used in marinades, dressings, sauces, pastes and rubs. For the best results, grind the spices just before making the preparation.

Some recipes call for whole spices to be dry-roasted before use, particularly in Indian cooking. This concentrates the flavour and also makes the spices easier to grind. Heat a heavy-based pan on a medium heat until it feels hot when you hold your hand above the base, tip in the spices, then stir or shake the pan constantly.

The spices will darken, smoke a little and release their aroma. Lower the heat so they don't burn; a tablespoon of spices will be ready in around two to three minutes, but a large amount can take several minutes to brown evenly. Tip the roasted spices into a bowl and leave to cool before grinding them.

> **If spices are added at the beginning of cooking their flavour will spread through the dish**

If a recipe calls for frying spices, have all the other ingredients ready before starting because spices fry quickly. Use a heavy pan, heat the oil until a light haze rises, quickly tip in the spices – whole ones first – and use them in the sequence given in the recipe. They will sizzle and brown, but don't let them burn.

Remember that if spices are added at the beginning of cooking their flavour will spread through the dish, but if they're stirred through at the end of cooking then their aroma will be emphasised in the dish. Some spice blends are made using whole spices, which should be tied together in a muslin bag before adding to a pan of poaching liquid.

Most blends are mixtures of ground spices. Always make these in small quantities – don't try to save time by making a large batch and storing most of it, unless you know you will use it again soon. Some common spice blend recipes can be found on p59. If you buy ready-made spice mixtures then purchase small amounts, and store in a small, dark container.

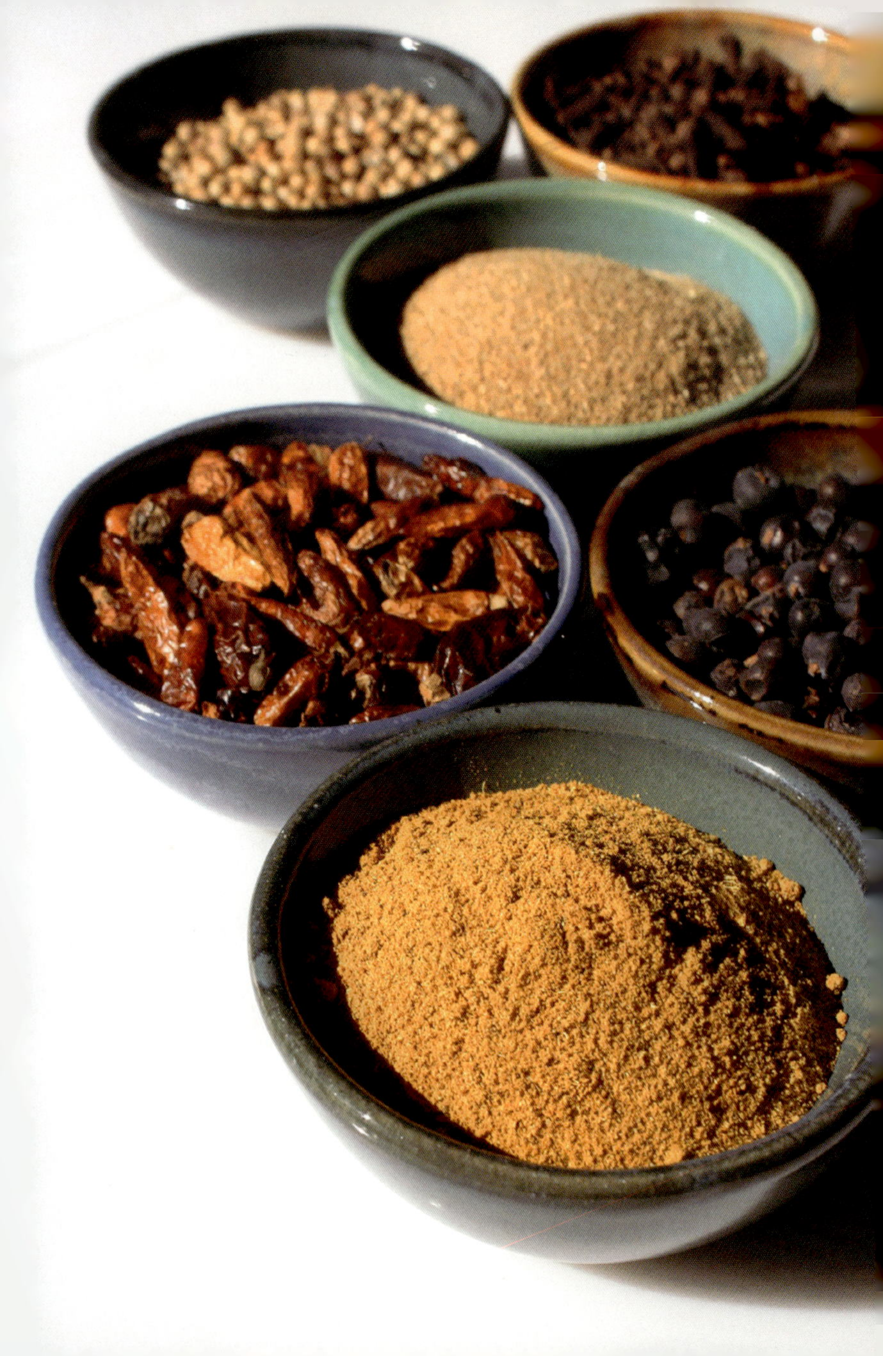

2. The history of spices

The story of how spices became part of our everyday diet involves a journey that spans continents and millennia

Many tales of romance and mythology are associated with spices, but the history of spices is essentially a history of trade – of fortunes and empires made and lost, of bloodshed, piracy and greed. The most important spice plants are native to tropical Asia and have been traded there for millennia. Cassia is mentioned in *Pen Ts'ao Ching*, a herbal medicine book written around 2700 BCE. Nutmeg and cloves were traded to China before 300 BCE, when officers of state put cloves in their mouths to sweeten their breath when addressing the emperor.

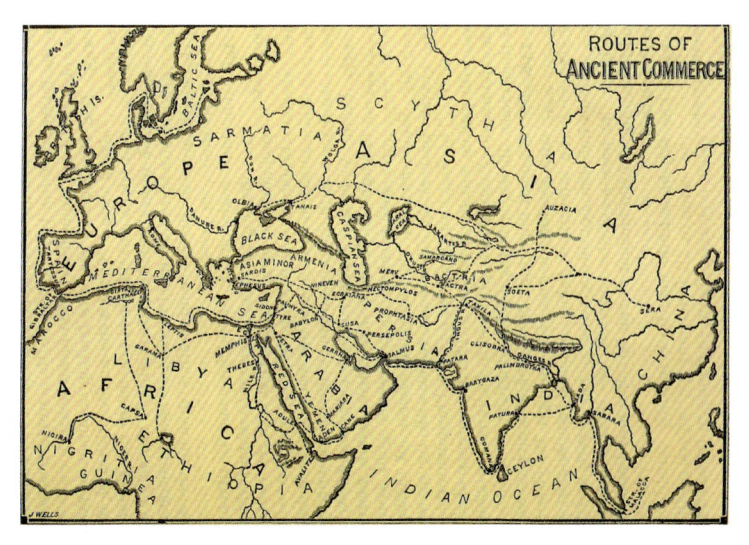

> **In India, spices such as pepper, turmeric, cardamom and ginger have been used for thousands of years in medicine and cooking**

Cuneiform records include spices and herbs used in the Tigris and Euphrates valleys, and a scroll from the reign of King Ashurbanipal of Assyria (668-633 BCE) records several aromatic plants, including cardamom, coriander, cumin, myrrh, saffron and turmeric. In India, spices such as pepper, turmeric, cardamom and ginger have been used for thousands of years in medicine and cooking. The Egyptians used spices for embalming, body ointments and to fumigate their homes, while the Ebers Papyrus (circa 1550 BCE) mentions aromatics including cardamom, cassia, coriander and saffron.

Trade routes
The trade routes between India, Indonesia and China were established long before any trade westwards. In affluent Asian societies, spices were used regularly in medicine and cooking, and pepper and other spices left India's Malabar coast for China in exchange for porcelain and silk.

Indian traders took spices and textiles to the Persian Gulf to sell to Arab traders, who remained the middlemen in the European trade with Asia and sub-Saharan Africa for centuries. To preserve their monopoly they spread alarming tales to discourage customers from attempting to find the sources of their prized merchandise.

Founded by Alexander the Great in 332 BCE, the city of Alexandria soon became a great trading centre between East and West. Several overland trade routes were established to bring spices and other oriental luxuries to the West. The earliest sea route was from the Malabar coast of India to the Persian Gulf, round the coast of Arabia and up the Red Sea.

The Romans started sailing to India from Egypt in the first century CE. It was a long voyage, until Hippalus, a Greek sailor, discovered the monsoon winds. Ships sailed out with the southwest monsoon winds from April to October and returned with the northeast monsoons from October to April.

These fast voyages enabled Rome to break the Arab stranglehold. They used spices extravagantly in cooking, perfume, cosmetics and medicine. In return, a steady flow of gold went east to pay for the silks, precious stones and spices.

Rome to the Middle Ages
Pepper, ginger and turmeric were the most commonly used spices in Rome. Apicius' recipes in *De Re Coquinaria* included spices to preserve food, enhance its flavour and aid digestion, and Roman armies took spices with them as they conquered Europe. When the Goths besieged Rome in 408 CE, they knew well the value of spices and other luxuries. After the fall of Rome, some spices reached Europe, but for 400 years there was little contact between Muslim Arabs and Christian Europe.

While Europe lapsed into the Dark Ages, the Abbasid dynasty established a thriving civilisation in Baghdad, with physicians and pharmacologists creating techniques to distil essential oils from plants and extract scents from flowers and herbs. Their food was flavoured with rosewater, saffron, cinnamon, coriander, nutmeg, mace and ginger.

European trade resumed in the 11th century with the crusades. During this time, spices and other oriental goods became more

> **In 1180, Henry II established the Peppers' Guild in London, and peppercorns were used to pay taxes and rent**

widely available beyond the palaces of state and church.

In 1180, Henry II established the Peppers' Guild in London, the city's first mercantile guild. Peppercorns were used to pay taxes and rent, and kings and princes throughout Europe levied taxes on spices. However, accounts from monasteries and noble households show the lavish use of spices continued.

The crusaders' supplies came from Venice and Genoa, the main seafarers of the Mediterranean. Venice defeated Genoa in 1380 and had an unprecedented trade boom for the next 100

A Chinese spice cabinet

years, supplying Europe with spices, silks and jewels and Asia with saffron, wool, gold and silver.

New routes
The Portuguese and the Spaniards were determined to find other routes to the East to break the Venetian monopoly. Vasco da Gama reached Calicut via the Cape of Good Hope in 1498, and returned with spices and precious stones. The trade passed to Lisbon, and for the next century the Portuguese supplied spices to Europe at even higher prices than those of the Venetians. They settled in Asian trading towns and on the Spice Islands. When the last ship of Magellan's fleet arrived in the Moluccas in 1522, after sailing westwards round the globe under the flag of Spain, the two countries were rivals in the islands until they were united under the Spanish crown in 1580.

Meanwhile, the Dutch, who had been trading spices from Lisbon into northern Europe, decided to organise their own journey to the Indies. A group of Amsterdam merchants financed an expedition in 1595, which returned with supplies of pepper, nutmeg and mace. In 1602, the Vereenigde Oost-Indische Compagnie (Dutch East India Company) was formed.

The Dutch proved a superior naval force to the Portuguese, and were even more ruthless in their treatment of the native population and in protecting their monopoly. The spice crops outstripped demand, and huge quantities of spices were burned in Amsterdam to maintain prices in Europe. The cost was immense, and by the 18th century the trade unprofitable.

The English came late to the Asian trade. In 1609, James I granted the East India Company the monopoly. However, monopolies were about to end.

In 1770, the aptly named Pierre Poivre, a French botanist, smuggled clove and nutmeg trees to Isle de France (Mauritius). More plantings were made in tropical colonies, including the West Indies, and by the 19th century prices had fallen.

Columbus made landfall on Hispaniola six years before Vasco da Gama reached the East. He made four voyages west, searching for the fabled riches of the East. Instead, he returned with tobacco, kidney beans, capsicums and allspice. Cortés conquered Mexico in 1519 and returned to Spain with many other foods, including vanilla, and gold and silver.

> Migration has also played a significant role in the spread of spices over the years

Migration

Another factor that has played a significant role in the spread of spices over the years is migration. Immigrant communities, whether established by colonial force or economic plight, took their traditional ingredients and cooking methods and combined them with local produce.

These are the origins of Cape Malay and Cape Indian dishes, as well as Cajun cooking, the use of Colombo powder in the French West Indies, the 'rijsttafel' of Holland, Japanese dishes in Peru and, of course, the curries of the UK.

3. An A-Z of spices

The characteristics of some of the most common spices, and how they are used in different cuisines all over the world

In the past decade or two there has been a surge in interest in spices as people travel more and learn about local cuisines. Restaurants and cookery books bring those cooking styles to their towns and cities, and this, in turn, creates a demand for special ingredients, particularly spices. Dishes now travel the world as we cook Malay or Peruvian or Swedish meals at home. This chapter explores the characteristics of some common spices and how they are used in different cuisines. Each spice has been put into a broad flavour category to serve as a guide, but their aromas and flavours are more complex – and interpretations are subjective.

Spice character key
● Acidic
● Anise
● Bitter
● Citrus
● Earthy
● Fruity
● Nutty
● Pungent
● Sweet
● Warm
● Woody

AKUDJURA ●
Solanum centrale

Akudjura is native to the Australian desert, which explains why it is also commonly known as bush tomato, or desert raisin. Aboriginal people have long gathered the fruits for staple food stores; now, large quantities are sent to spice merchants and condiment-makers in the cities.

Fruits left to dry on the plant shrink to grape size, turn chocolate brown and acquire a chewy texture. Dehydration concentrates the flavours. The aroma suggests caramel-chocolate with sun-dried tomato; they taste of caramel and tamarillo with a refreshing, sharp aftertaste. Whole bush tomatoes should be soaked for 20-30 minutes before use. The ground fruit, always called akudjura, may be orange-red or brown.

Uses: Use akudjura instead of sweet paprika or sun-dried tomato. Sprinkle on salads, egg dishes and steamed vegetables. It is also used in relishes and chutneys, and can be mixed with coriander, wattle and lemon myrtle for a fine meat marinade.

ALLSPICE ● ●
Pimienta dioica

Native to tropical Central America and the Caribbean islands, allspice was brought to Europe by Columbus. He thought he had found pepper, hence its Spanish name *pimiento*. The best quality allspice comes from Jamaica.

The name evokes its warm, fragrant aroma – a compound of nutmeg, cloves and cinnamon; the pungent taste reflects the same tones with notes of pepper. The flavour is in the shell rather than the seeds it contains. Unripe berries are dried in the sun; the dried red-brown berries resemble large peppercorns, with a wrinkly shell.

Uses: Fresh allspice leaves are used in Caribbean cuisine to flavour soups and stews, in jerk seasoning, and with chicken and fish dishes. Allspice has both sweet and savoury uses. It is used in mincemeat, spiced biscuits and fruit pies, and goes well with pineapple. It is also a good flavouring for soused herrings and spiced beef. Much of the world crop goes to the food industry for ketchups, pastrami, charcuterie and meat pies. Try allspice with aubergines, squash, sweet potatoes and other root vegetables. It combines well with chilli, coriander, ginger and thyme.

ANISE ● ●
Pimpinella anisum

Native to the Middle East and the eastern Mediterranean, anise is now grown around the world. Anise was originally used medicinally, and it was the Romans who introduced anise-spiced cakes to aid digestion after a rich meal.

Both the aroma and taste of anise are sweet, warm and liquorice-like, and more subtle than fennel or star anise. The leaves have a similarly fragrant, liquorice flavour. Indian aniseed can have a bitter note.

Uses: In India and the Middle East anise is used in breads, vegetable and seafood dishes, and seeds fried in oil garnish pulses. In Europe it is often used in sweet cakes, biscuits, fruit dishes and confectionery. It flavours Scandinavian rye breads, Mediterranean fish stews and Catalonian cakes of dried figs and almonds.

ANNATTO ● ●
Bixa orellana

Annatto comes from the orange-red seeds of a small evergreen tree found throughout the Caribbean, South and Central America. It produces spiky orange-brown fruits, each containing around 50 angular, red seeds encased in pulp. It is sometimes known by the Spanish name *achiote*.

Ripe fruits are harvested, split open and macerated in water. The pulp is pressed into cakes for processing into dyes and the seeds are dried as a spice. In pre-Columbian times many tribes used annatto as body paint; today it is widely used as a natural food dye in cheeses, butter, custard and smoked fish. Annatto has a light, flowery scent and a slightly bitter, earthy taste.

Uses: Many Central and South American dishes use annatto for its distinctive yellow-orange colour. In Peru annatto colours a marinade for spiced pork; it is essential to the Yucatecan marinade for pork or chicken baked in a pit oven. In Filippino cooking it is mostly used to colour soups and stews. Annatto is good with egg dishes, salt cod, pulses and most vegetables. It combines well with garlic, chillies, oregano and paprika.

ASAFOETIDA ● ●
Ferula species

Asafoetida is a dried, resinous gum exuded from the rhizome of several species of *ferula*, which are fetid-smelling perennials native to Iran and Afghanistan, now mostly cultivated in northern India. Asafoetida's sulphurous smell is transformed by cooking to become pleasantly onion-like.

The Romans imported it from Persia. Apicius recommended keeping a small piece in a jar of pine nuts to impregnate them. A few crushed pine nuts were added to the dish, and the jar topped up with more nuts. Today, asafoetida is important for the Brahmin and Jain sects, whose diet forbids the use of garlic and onions. It is essential in Indian sambhar powder (see p62).

It is sold in solid or powdered form; the best quality is sold as "tears" (small individual pieces) or "lumps" (tears that have been processed into a mass).

Uses: Asafoetida flavours pulses, pickles, sauces and relishes. It is good with fresh fish and grilled meat – rub a piece on the grill before cooking. It should always be used sparingly – a pinch of powder or a crushed piece of a tear will flavour a dish.

CARAWAY ● ●
Carum carvi
Native to northern and central Europe and Asia, caraway is a hardy biennial umbellifer. The curved seeds are brown with lighter ridges and tapered ends. Their aroma is warm and bittersweet – as is the flavour, which also has a sharp note.

The Romans flavoured vegetables with caraway, and in medieval recipes it is used with bean and cabbage dishes. In Shakespeare's *Henry IV, Part 2* Shallow invites Falstaff to his orchard, "where in an arbour we will eat a last year's pippin… with a dish of caraway". Caraway remained popular with apples and other fruits, and it also became fashionable to coat the seeds with sugar syrup to make comfits, served to aid digestion at the end of a meal.

Uses: English seed cake is still made; in central and northern Europe caraway is used to flavour rye breads, sausages, sauerkraut and coleslaw. It goes well with rich meats such as pork and goose. Hungary has a traditional caraway soup, and caraway figures in goulash. In Alsace it accompanies Munster cheese; in Germany it flavours Kümmel and in Scandinavia aquavit.

CARDAMOM ● ●
Elletaria cardamomum
The third most expensive spice, after saffron and vanilla, this member of the ginger family is native to the rain forests of the Western Ghats in India. Cardamom plants grow slowly, the yield

is tiny, and pods are harvested by hand – all of which explains the high price. The aroma is sweetish and mellow yet pungent, the taste fruity, warm and bittersweet.

Cardamom has been used for medicinal purposes in India for thousands of years. The Moghuls used cardamom as a breath freshener, and it reached the Mediterranean along the caravan routes, where it was primarily used in perfumes. In Europe in the 17th century it was used to flavour mead – "cardamom seeds mingled with the suspended spices, adde much to the pleasantness of the drink", *The Closet Opened*, Sir Kenelm Digby, 1669.

Uses: In India, cardamom goes into curry and masala blends, daals and pilafs. In the Middle East it is used in spice blends and to flavour coffee, and also sweets. Scandinavians use cardamom in breads, cakes and biscuits, as well as pickled herring, meatballs and sausages. Use cardamom with root vegetables and squash, baked apples, poached pears and poached chicken. It combines well with cinnamon, cloves, coriander, ginger, pepper and saffron.

CASSIA ● ●
Cinnamomum cassia

The dried bark of a species of laurel that is native to Assam and northern Burma and is now cultivated in southern China and Vietnam, cassia is similar to cinnamon, but less fine. The bark is coarser, rough and greyish-brown on the outside; the inner bark is lighter and smooth.

In many countries cassia and cinnamon are used interchangeably, and in the US cassia is preferred. Its warm, woody aroma is more pronounced than that of cinnamon because its volatile oil content is higher, and the taste is sweetish with a bitter, astringent edge.

Cassia buds look rather like small cloves. They are in fact the dried, unripe fruits. The hard, red-brown seed is just visible in the wrinkled calyx. They have a warm, cinnamon-like aroma; their musky, sweetish flavour is less pungent than that of the bark.
Uses: Cassia is widely used in Chinese braised dishes and is a constituent of Chinese five-spice powder (p59). In India it is used in some masalas, curries and pilafs. Its pungency makes it better suited than cinnamon to rich meats such as pork, and it is a good flavouring for squashes and pulses. Use a piece to flavour mulled wine.

CHILLIES
Capsicum species
Native to Central and South America and the Caribbean islands, chillies had been cultivated there for thousands of years before the arrival of the Spaniards, who introduced them to the rest of the world. Chillies are now the world's biggest spice crop;

hundreds of varieties are grown throughout the tropics and eaten daily by at least a quarter of the world's population.

They come in all shapes, colours and sizes, from tiny and pointy to 30cm long. Large, fleshy chillies tend to be milder than small, thin-skinned ones. *C chinense* are the hottest, *C frutescens* come next and *C annuum* are the mildest. Chillies stimulate the appetite not merely with pungency, but also with floral, fruity, smoky, tobacco or liquorice flavours. A good source of vitamins A and C, they pep up the diet of millions of people who daily eat bland staples.

The pungency derives from capsaicin in the seeds, veins and skin and the content varies according to the type of chilli and its ripeness. Removing the seeds and veins reduces the heat. Capsaicin stimulates the digestive process, which induces perspiration and has a cooling effect on the body.

The heat scale of chillies is from 1 for mild to 10 for extremely hot. Ground chilli is produced from dried red chillies; many brands are hot rather than flavourful (7-9/10). Chilli flakes are produced from milder chillies (2-6/10). In Hungary, Turkey and the Middle East these are used as a table condiment; in Japan and Korea hotter flakes are common.

Cayenne, the most common powdered chilli, is pungent and slightly smoky (8/10). Other chilli powders are often a blend of ground chilli and other spices (1-3/10). Good quality ground chilli smells fruity and earthy and contains small traces of oils that will stain the fingers slightly.

Uses: Chillies are used in several spice mixtures, powders and pastes such as harissa (p60), jerk seasoning (p61), kimchi, moles and nam prik. Hundreds of chilli oils, pastes, powders and sauces are produced worldwide. See also paprika (p41).

CINNAMON ● ●
*Cinnamomum verum,
C zelanicum*

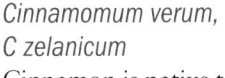

Cinnamon is native to Sri Lanka and, like cassia, is a member of the laurel family. Strips of paper-thin bark are rolled one into another to form slender quills, which are dried gently in the shade. When small quantities of cinnamon reached Europe it was one of the essential luxuries of the rich, along with ginger, galangal, nutmeg, cloves and pepper.

Cinnamon has a warm, woody aroma that is delicate yet intense; the taste is fragrant, with notes of clove and citrus. The presence of eugenol in the essential oil distinguishes cinnamon from cassia, providing the note of clove.

Uses: Suited to both savoury and sweet dishes, cinnamon is good with lamb and fruit in tagines. It flavours Indian pilafs, masalas and condiments. It goes well with almonds, apples and bananas, gives a subtle spiced note to many cakes and desserts, and makes a fine ice cream. Combine it with cloves, cardamom, cumin and tamarind.

CLOVES ● ●
Syzium aromaticum

Cloves are the dried, immature flower buds of an evergreen tree of the myrtle family, native to the Moluccas. The Chinese were among the first to appreciate cloves, having used them from the third century BCE to sweeten the breath. Excavations in the Euphrates valley revealed charred cloves dating back to 3000 BCE.

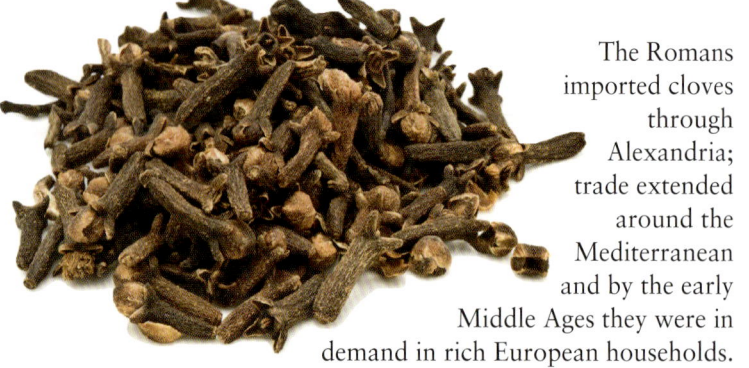

The Romans imported cloves through Alexandria; trade extended around the Mediterranean and by the early Middle Ages they were in demand in rich European households.

Cloves have an assertive, warm, peppery aroma; if tasted alone a clove is fruity, yet sharp and bitter. It leaves a numbing sensation in the mouth, which is why chewing a clove was a remedy for toothache. The flavour is tempered by cooking.

Uses: Cloves are used to flavour baked goods, desserts and preserves, pickles and syrups. Stick a clove into an onion to flavour a pot of lentils, or use them in mulled wine. In Holland they flavour Nagelkaas; in America hams are glazed and studded with cloves. Used in many spice blends, cloves are essential to garam masala (p60), five-spice powder (p59) and quatre-épices (p61). Cloves combine well with cardamom, cinnamon and, more surprisingly, with chocolate.

CORIANDER ● ●
Coriandrum sativum

Coriander, both as a herb and a spice, is a fragrant staple of many cuisines. It is grown worldwide for its seed, leaves and roots. However, many people do not find the leaves "fragrant" at all, rather they find the aroma unpleasant. In *Theatrum Botanicum* (1640) John Parkinson called it "a strong and loathsome savour scarce to be endured".

Coriander seeds have a sweet, floral-woody aroma with peppery tones, while the taste is mellow and warm, with a hint of orange peel.

Coriander seed has a long and varied culinary history. It was one of the foods found in Tutankhamen's tomb, it was used extensively in Greek and Roman cooking, and in al-Baghdadi's tenth-century cookbook cinnamon and coriander are the two most frequently used spices.

Uses: In Europe and America the coriander flavour can be detected in many pickles and chutneys; French vegetables *à la grecque* are flavoured with coriander, as are crushed green olives from Cyprus. Use it with oranges and rhubarb, with mushrooms, cauliflower and carrots, with poultry and pork.

The leaves are essential in Latin American, Portuguese and Asian cooking, where they are used prolifically in soups and stir-fried dishes. In Mexico coriander leaves are combined with chillies, garlic and lime juice in salsas. Peruvian cooks use coriander, chillies and local herbs in an assertive table sauce.

CUMIN ● ●
Cuminum cyminum

Native to the Nile Valley and the eastern Mediterranean, cumin has long been cultivated in many warm climates. Used as a spice, a medicine and a preservative, seeds have been found in archaeological sites in Egypt and in Crete. The Greeks and Romans used cumin liberally. Widely used across medieval Europe, in England cumin was recorded as a taxable import in 1419. Cumin was primarily a remedy for indigestion and flatulence; the rich preferred dishes flavoured with costly nutmeg, ginger and cinnamon.

Cumin seeds are pale brown or greyish, and ridged. The intense, earthy aroma has a warm, spicy-sweet note; the flavour is slightly bitter, earthy and pungent.

Uses: Cumin is sometimes used alone, as in Dutch Leidsekaas or Alsatian pretzels, but more frequently in combination with other flavourings. Chilli con carne, couscous, merguez, falafel, many masalas, curry pastes and spice blends include cumin. In India it continues to be used as a digestive aid and remedy for diarrhoea.

CURRY LEAVES ● ●
Murraya koenigii

Curry leaves come from an attractive small tree that grows wild throughout India and in Sri Lanka. Trees have long been cultivated in domestic gardens for culinary use; now there are also commercial plantations, including some in Malaysia and Australia. Fresh leaves can be bought in small bundles from Asian grocers and can be stored in a plastic container in the fridge for seven to ten days or in the freezer for a couple of months. Avoid dried leaves.

Rubbed and bruised leaves give off an intense musky, spicy aroma; the taste is pleasantly warm, lemony and slightly bitter.

Uses: Curry leaves are used in the fish dishes of Kerala and Chennai. Much south Indian cooking is vegetarian and curry leaves give depth to these dishes. Sometimes leaves are fried with mustard seeds, asafoetida or onion to provide the basic flavouring at the start of the cooking process. This combination may also be added at the end, as the essential tadka to pour over lentil dishes. Curry leaves impart a delicate, spicy flavour to curries without the heat associated with other spices. Indian emigrants took curry leaves to South Africa and made them an important ingredient of Tamil cooking there.

DILL ●
Anethum graveolens

The name dill comes from old Norse "dilla", meaning to soothe. Pliny noted that "dill allays gripings of the stomach", a view held by herbalists today.

An annual plant, dill is grown for its leaves (often called dill weed) and its seeds. The feathery leaves have a pleasant aroma of anise and lemon; the taste is of parsley and anise. The seeds smell rather like sweet caraway; they have a more robust flavour than the herb, and leave a warm sensation in the mouth.

Uses: Dill seeds are good with root vegetables, pumpkins and squashes. In some countries they are used in breads and pastries. In spice blends with fenugreek and cumin they liven up lentil dishes. Both seeds and leaves are used in pickling, and the herb is used to make Scandinavian gravlax. It also marries well with beetroot, broad beans, cucumber, eggs, rice and yogurt.

FENNEL ● ●
Foeniculum vulgare

A tall, graceful perennial native to the Mediterranean, fennel is one of the oldest cultivated plants, now grown throughout the temperate regions of the world. The whole plant is aromatic, with a liquorice-anise aroma and taste. Both its feathery leaves and seeds are used in the kitchen. In recent years fennel pollen – an intensely flavoured golden-green dust – has become fashionable. Its rarity means it commands a very high price.

Uses: Fennel is the traditional flavouring for fish; early cookery books recommend fennel sauce to accompany oily fish such as salmon and mackerel. In Provence sea bass and red mullet are grilled over fennel stalks. The Italians use the seed to flavour pork and the finocchiona of Florence. Fennel seeds are added to breads, pickles and soups; they flavour sauerkraut, and go well with lentils, cabbage and potatoes. Chopped leaves or a few flowers will give an anise taste to cold soups, fish chowders or grilled fish.

In Indian and Malay cooking the seeds are usually dry roasted, which brings out their sweetness. Fennel is used in Bengali panch phoron (p61), and is a constituent of Chinese five-spice powder (p59).

FENUGREEK ●
Trigonella foenum-graecum

Trigonella refers to the triangular shape of fenugreek flowers, and *foenum-graecum* means Greek hay. In ancient times fenugreek was grown as cattle fodder. Its medicinal properties were recorded in Egyptian times, when it was also used in embalming.

A member of the pea family, fenugreek's curved seedpods resemble miniature beans, and the yellow-brown seeds can be likened to tiny pebbles. Their sharp, spicy aroma is reminiscent of curry powder; the flavour celery-like with a bitter note. Brief dry roasting gives seeds a pleasant nutty, maple-syrup taste. Fresh leaves are mildly astringent; they are good in salads, and the seeds are easily sprouted.

Uses: Also sold under its Indian name, *methi*, fenugreek is widely used in Indian vegetarian cooking. It is a good source of proteins, vitamins and minerals. Fresh leaves are cooked as a vegetable; they are chopped and added to chapattis and naans. In Iran, leaves are essential to qhormeh sabzi, a classic herb stew.

Seeds are combined with other spices in sambar powder (p62) and panch phoron (p61).

GALANGAL ● ●
Alpinia species

The several varieties of galangal are all members of the ginger family. The most important is greater galangal (*Alpinia galanga*), native to Java. Galangal reached Europe in the Middle Ages and was esteemed for medicinal and culinary purposes. It is still used in Ayurvedic and Chinese medicine.

Galangal was popular in medieval kitchens. Chaucer's cook in *The Canterbury Tales* (1386) had "poudre marchant tart and galyngale" to flavour his chickens. Subsequently it lost favour in Europe, until recent interest in Asian dishes created new demand. The orange-brown, knobbly rhizomes are fibrous and tougher than ginger unless very young. The gingery aroma is penetrating, the taste sharp. Dried galangal is available sliced and as a sandy beige powder with a sourish aroma and a mild ginger flavour.

Uses: Throughout Southeast Asia fresh rhizomes are used in soups, curries, sambals, spice pastes and sauces. In Thai and Malay cooking it is often preferred to ginger, to neutralise the smell of fish and seafood. The dried root, first soaked in hot water, can be used in soups and stews, but should be removed before serving.

GINGER ● ●
Zingiber officinale

Ginger is a lush, tropical plant with lance-like leaves. The rhizomes supply the spice. It has been cultivated in India and southern China for thousands of years, as a spice in cooking and also for its wide-ranging medicinal properties. Ginger arrived in the 3rd century BCE in Japan and Korea and was used in medicine and in cooking.

In Asia, ginger has always been used fresh, except in spice mixtures; in Europe only dried was known, as fresh could not be transported. Dioscorides praised ginger's medicinal qualities, while the Romans esteemed its culinary virtues.

Fresh ginger has a warm aroma with a refreshing woody note and sweet citrus undertones. The flavour is tangy and has bite. Powdered ginger is warm and pungent with lemony notes, the taste fiery and penetrating.

Fresh rhizomes should be hard and heavy with a smooth, taut skin. Very young, creamy white ginger is occasionally found in oriental shops in early summer. Fragrant and mild, it can be sliced and stir-fried. Dry ginger can be bought as pieces of rhizome, in slices or as powder.

Uses: Ginger is a versatile spice. In Asia fresh ginger is often combined with garlic, lemongrass, chilli and coriander. The Chinese use it with fish, meat and poultry to neutralise odours. The Japanese also use it to mask fishy smells; freshly grated ginger is often used in dipping sauces for tempura. Gari (pickled, sliced young ginger) is served with sushi and sashimi as a digestive condiment.

Korean kimchi relies on ginger and garlic for its flavour. Some Indian dishes are based on an onion, ginger and garlic paste that flavours the oil or ghee before other ingredients are added.

Preserved ginger and crystallized ginger are eaten as sweetmeats or used to flavour sweet sauces, ice cream, pastries and cakes. In western kitchens dried ginger has long been a popular baking spice. In the Mahgreb it is used in couscous and tagines. It is an essential ingredient of quatre-épices (p61), five-spice powder (p59), ras el hanout (p61) and pickling spice.

GOLPAR ● ●
Heracleum persicum

Golpar is an Iranian spice, the seed of a species of giant hogweed, sometimes erroneously described as angelica or marjoram seed. The seeds are yellow-green with brown markings; they can be bought whole or ground from Iranian shops and a few spice merchants. The aroma is earthy and herbaceous, and the flavour pungent, yet also mellow, with a bitter note that diminishes during cooking. In Persian cooking it is considered a "warm" food to balance "cold" foods.

Uses: Ground seed is sprinkled over broad beans, lentils, mushrooms and potatoes; it is used to flavour soups, stews and rice dishes. Golpar is also popular sprinkled over pomegranate as a snack, and in yogurt or labneh. Combined with salt it makes an interesting seasoning, golpar namak. Whole seeds are used in many Iranian pickles.

GRAINS OF PARADISE ● ●
Aframomum melegueta

Grains of paradise are the seeds of a reed-like plant, related to cardamom, indigenous to the tropical coast of West Africa. Originally called Guinea pepper or melegueta pepper, the seeds were transported in caravans across the Sahel and the Sahara to Europe, where they were readily accepted, long before the Portuguese developed the maritime trade and sold them as "grains of paradise" to enhance their value.

Grains of paradise feature in recipes for a black sauce for capons and for hippocras in *The Forme of Cury*, compiled in 1390 by Richard II's master cook, and also appear in *Le Ménagier de Paris* of the same period. Grains of paradise continued to be used to spice wines and beer; hot sack was a popular 17th-century tonic.

The small, red-brown seeds resemble tiny blunt pyramids contained in a wrinkled, brown, fig-shaped capsule. When crushed the white flesh inside is revealed. The flavour is complex and peppery, with ginger, cardamom and fruity notes and a hint of cloves. Little used now in Europe, grains of paradise deserve to be better known.

Uses: Use them instead of pepper, or combined with other spices – allspice, cinnamon, cloves and nutmeg – to make your own blend. They are important in two North African spices mixtures – qâlat daqqa (p61) and ras el hanout (p61).

JUNIPER ●
Juniperus communis

Juniper is a prickly small tree of the cypress family that grows wild throughout the northern hemisphere. The female trees bear berries that take two to three years to ripen into the purple-blue fruit. Picking is hazardous because of the sharp, spiky leaves. Berries are soft when picked and retain some softness when dried. Those picked in warmer areas have a stronger bitter-sweet aroma. The taste is refreshing and sweet, with notes of resin and pine.

Juniper is the principal flavouring for gin. Genever was first produced in Holland in the 16th century, and initially used for medicinal purposes. Its popularity grew in England when William of Orange became king in the 17th century.

Uses: Juniper is a natural foil for game and fatty meats. It combines well with garlic, allspice and aromatic herbs. Scandinavians use it in marinades for game and pork. In Belgium and northern France it flavours venison and pâtés, and sauerkraut in Germany and Alsace. Salt, garlic and crushed berries make a good rub for venison and game birds. As well as being a key ingredient in gin, Juniper is widely used to flavour cordials, spirits and other drinks, including a Finnish rye beer.

LEMONGRASS •
Cymbopogon citratus
A tall grass native to tropical Asia, lemongrass is now cultivated in Australia, South America and West Africa. The bulbous base of the plant is aromatic and distinctly citrus-like. It has a high citral content, also found in lemon peel. The flavour is refreshingly clean, tart and lemony with peppery notes.

Freeze-dried lemongrass keeps its flavour reasonably well, but air-dried lemongrass loses its essential oils. Use lemon rind or ground lemon myrtle leaves instead. If lemongrass is to be eaten, discard the top of the stem and the outer layers, then cut the base into fine rings.

Uses: Lemongrass gives a fresh, subtle, lemony flavour to many South Asian dishes and combines well with Asian basils, coriander, garlic, ginger, shallots and chillies. The coarse outer leaves must be removed and they can make a refreshing tea. The inner stem is added whole to a soup or stew and removed before serving. Lemongrass is widely used in the nonya cooking of Singapore, in Vietnamese salads and spring rolls, and in Thai hot and sour soups. Increasingly, its elusive flavour turns up in western dishes. It goes well with fish and seafood, especially mussels; try adding it to stock for poaching chicken or fish.

LEMON MYRTLE ●
Backhousia citriodora

The lemon myrtle tree, native to the coastal rain forests of Queensland, is the source of this popular Australian spice. Trees have been introduced into southern Europe, South Africa and parts of the USA, but its culinary potential has not yet been recognised outside Australia. Use fresh leaves if you have them, otherwise dried and powdered leaves are available. Buy leaves and grind them as needed because the powder quickly loses its essential oils.

Uses: This versatile spice can be used whenever lemongrass or lemon zest is called for, because lemon myrtle is the richest known source of citral. The aroma of lemon and lime is pronounced when the leaves are crushed. Lemon myrtle's flavour is stronger still, resembling lemon zest, but there is a lingering aftertaste of eucalyptus.

Use sparingly and cook lemon myrtle briefly or the agreeable lemon taste is lost. It is well-suited to stir-fried dishes and fishcakes and can be sprinkled onto fish or chicken to be grilled or barbecued. Try it with rice, or stir a little into mayonnaise or yogurt. It combines well with akudjura, cardamom, chillies, ginger and parsley.

MAKRUT LIME ●
Citrus hystrix

The small, evergreen makrut lime tree is native to Southeast Asia and until relatively recently was little known outside that region. Now it is cultivated in Australia, Florida and California.

The leathery leaves grow in an unusual double form, as two on a single petiole, resembling wings. When torn or cut they release a vibrant floral and citrus aroma. Both aroma and flavour are assertive yet delicate. Fresh leaves, now widely available in Thai shops, are much better than frozen or dried. Makrut lime zest is used in small amounts, often in curry pastes. It too is bitter with a citrus back note.

Uses: Makrut lime leaves and zest are used in kitchens throughout Southeast Asia. Lime leaves provide the tangy citrus aromas of soups, salads, curries and fish dishes. Add whole leaves to soups and stews, and remove before serving. If the leaves are to be eaten, shred them to fine threads. Leaves combine well with Asian basils, cardamom, chilli, galangal, ginger, lemongrass and star anise.

MASTIC ●
Pistacia lentiscus

The use of mastic dates back to classical times. Hippocrates recommended it for digestive problems and as a breath freshener.

The Greek island of Chios is renowned for its lentisk trees from which mastic is taken. The evergreen trees produce a sticky resin from around six years old. The trunks

Spice character key
- ● Acidic
- ● Anise
- ● Bitter
- ● Citrus
- ● Earthy
- ● Fruity
- ● Nutty
- ● Pungent
- ● Sweet
- ● Warm
- ● Woody

are cut in late summer to allow the resin to ooze out and harden into oval or oblong shapes, which are collected, washed and left to dry. Called tears because of their shape, they are light gold in colour and translucent. Mastic production is expensive and time-consuming, so the spice is expensive.

It has a light pine aroma, and the taste is mineral-like, slightly bitter, yet mouth freshening, which explains why it was the earliest form of chewing gum.

Uses: In the kitchen its main use is in baking, in sweetmeats and desserts. Mastic is used to flavour breads, pastries and desserts in Greece and Cyprus; it is essential to Turkish delight and gives an agreeable, lightly chewy texture to ice creams. Pounded to a powder, it combines well with cardamom, cinnamon, nigella and sesame, as well as pistachio nuts, walnuts, orange flower water and rosewater.

MUSTARD ●
Brassica species

Mustard is the main temperate zone spice crop. The seeds of two varieties are grown commercially for the kitchen. White mustard, *Sinapsis alba/B alba*, has long grown wild in the Middle East, North America and Europe. Its relatively mild, yellow seeds have good preservative properties. Brown mustard, *B juncea*, native to the foothills of the Himalayas, is bitter, hot and aromatic. Whole seeds have no aroma; when ground they are pungent.

Mustard is grown as a vegetable plant as well as for seed; fresh shoots are available as mustard and cress, and mizuna, Chinese red mustard and mustard greens are widely available.

Uses: Whole white seeds are primarily used in pickles and for marinades. In India whole brown seeds are fried in oil or ghee to give a nutty flavour and piquancy to a dish. Viscous mustard oil is widely used in Bengal.

Mustard powder keeps indefinitely, which is handy for adding a pinch to marinades and sauces. There are many blended mustards – some smooth, others with seeds. Many are flavoured with herbs, chillies, spices or fruits. The heat scale is largely determined by the liquid used.

The essential accompaniment to a hot dog or hamburger, American mustard is mild and sweet. Its bright yellow colour comes from turmeric. Dijon mustard is pale, smooth and clean tasting with a distinct nip, the classic mustard for sauces and dressings. Bordeaux is darker than Dijon, and is mild, slightly sweet and good with cheese and sausages. Meaux is grainy – the bite is followed by a rounded, mouth-filling taste. Try it with pork pies or gammon. German mustard is sweetish, often flavoured with dill or tarragon, and accompanies all German sausages.

NIGELLA ● ●
Nigella sativa
Related to the pretty garden plant love-in-a-mist, nigella is grown in western Asia and southern Europe for its seeds. The seeds are

"of a blackish colour, very like unto onion seed, in taste sharpe, and of an excellent sweet savour", *Herball*, Gerard (1597). When rubbed the seeds smell herbaceous, and the lingering flavour is nutty, earthy and peppery.

Uses: Popular in India, and essential to Bengali panch phoron (p61), nigella is used in breads, rice dishes, kormas and curries. In Iran it is a pickling spice, while in Lebanon it flavours kibbeh. Sprinkle over flatbreads or savoury pastries, alone or with sesame. Scatter over smashed or roast potatoes or other root vegetables, or stir into yogurt. Nigella combines well with cumin, coriander, allspice, thyme and savory.

NUTMEG and MACE ● ●
Myristica fragrans

"The nut… is as large as a small quince apple, having a similar rind and the same colour. Its first rind is as thick as the green rind of our walnut, and under that is a thin loose rind, under which is the mace, very red and wrapped about the rind of the nut, and inside this is the nutmeg." This description is from Antonio Pigafetta, a scholar who travelled with Magellan in 1519.

The small evergreen tree that produces mace and nutmeg is native to the Banda Islands of Indonesia. When the fruit splits open the mace is removed, pressed flat, quickly dried, then cured for a few months, until it becomes brittle and turns orange-yellow or red-orange. The seeds are dried in the sun for several weeks, until the nutmeg rattles within the outer shell. The shells are cracked open and the nutmegs graded by size.

The yield of nutmegs is about ten times higher than that of mace, which is why mace is more expensive. In 13th-century London mace cost 4s 7d a pound, the equivalent of three sheep. The availability of both spices increased in Europe after the

Portuguese conquest of the islands; in particular the use of nutmeg as both a medicine and a spice.

By the late 17th century it was the fashion for people to carry their own nutmegs and small silver or bone graters as a medical precaution and to flavour food, hot ale or possets.

Mace and nutmeg have a similar aroma and taste. Nutmeg is rich, fresh and warm, with sweet notes and a hint of clove. Mace has a stronger aroma of clove and pepper; the taste is warm, aromatic and subtle, with a light lemony sweetness.

Uses: In England nutmeg is used in milk puddings, fruit cakes and desserts. It goes well with many cheese dishes. The Dutch use it with cabbage, cauliflower and vegetable purées; the Italians in pasta sauces, with spinach and veal; the French add it to potato dishes. In Grenada (now the main producer) it makes a memorable syrup and a pepper sauce. Mace is primarily used in savoury foods, giving a delicate flavour to cheese dishes, seafood, veal and chicken, and it is essential to béchamel sauce.

A word of warning: in very large quantities, nutmeg is toxic, especially if accompanied by alcohol. Used in the quantities given in recipes, however, it is perfectly safe.

PAPRIKA ● ●
Capsicum annuum

Paprika is the name given to a range of vivid red powders made from dried large capsicums. Columbus brought capsicums as well as chillies from Central America. They were planted in monastery gardens, but it was much later that dried and ground bell peppers, *pimentón*, made an appearance in a cookery book.

Seeds reached Turkey via North Africa soon after they were planted in Spain. The Balkans and Hungary were part of the Ottoman Empire, and peppers were planted in Hungary.

Originally called Turkish pepper, the name paprika, adapted from Slavic names for pepper, came later.

There are many types of paprika, in varying shades from crimson to orange-brown. The aroma is restrained – some are smoky, others nose-prickling, and flavours vary from caramel, fruity and smoky notes to full-bodied, slightly bitter or mildly pungent. They range from 2-6/10 on the heat scale (see chillies, p21). Spain and Hungary produce the best paprika.

Uses: In Hungary paprika is the vibrant seasoning of goulash, paprikas and pôrkölt. It is also a table condiment. It is key to Spain's romesco sauce, and is widely used in slow-cooked dishes, with rice and potatoes, with fish, and in chorizo. In Morocco it flavours tagines and chermoula.

PEPPER ●
Piper nigrum

Pepper, the "king of spices", is the dried fruit of a vine native to the Western Ghats of Kerala. The history of the spice trade is bound up with the search for pepper; no other spice has dominated global trade or world cuisines. Once traded ounce for ounce for gold, it was a currency for paying rents and dowries. It reached Europe at least 3,000 years ago; the Greeks used pepper; the Romans sailed to India to find it and consumed large quantities. In volume and value it remains the most important spice.

> The history of the spice trade is bound up with the search for pepper; no other spice has dominated global trade or world cuisines

Today, the vines grow up support trees in the spice gardens, with the fruits hanging on tightly

AN A-Z OF SPICES

packed spikes. They are picked when they turn green and then left to dry in the sun.

When fully dried, the outer shell, containing piperine, becomes wrinkled and turns dark brown or black. Black pepper has a pungent, fruity, woody fragrance, and a lingering heat. The best black pepper comes from the Wyanad Valley in the Ghats.

White pepper is the core of the peppercorn; fruits are picked red, soaked to remove the outer skin, and dried. It lacks the aromatics of black pepper and is hotter and sharper. Indonesian Muntok is the best. Green peppercorns are immature fruits, preserved by freeze-drying or dehydration; lightly aromatic, they have an agreeable pungency.

The biggest producer of pepper now is Vietnam; it is also grown in Indonesia, Malaysia and Brazil. The flavour and heat vary because the piperine content changes according to where the pepper is grown.

Other peppers

Cubebs and long pepper were once as important as peppercorns, but now are seldom found except in India and Indonesia.

Pink pepper, *Schinus terebinthifolius*, is the fruit of the Brazilian pepper tree. Fruity, resinous and sweetly aromatic, it is similar to juniper.

Mountain pepper, *Tasmannia lancolata*, is from a tree native to Australia. Early colonists used the dried berries as a condiment. They are intensely pungent and numbing.

Uses: Pepper is the spice most widely used in Western kitchens; it rouses the appetite, its aromatic pungency combining well with most foods. Pepper brings out the flavours of other spices and keeps its own flavour when cooked.

POPPY ● ●
Papaver somniferum

Papaver somniferum means "sleep-inducing poppy", and in ancient cultures the narcotic latex that oozes from the unripe seed pods, when cut, was used as a sedative. The poppy has been cultivated for thousands of years for opium, and also for its ripe seeds. It is native to central Asia, but cultivation spread east to India and China; its valuable pain-reducing effects were an incentive to growing it. Unfortunately, abuse of opium has changed the way we view the poppy.

Nevertheless, the seeds, which have no narcotic properties, are still valued in the kitchen. Seeds can be dark blue (most commonly used in Europe) or white (as preferred in Asia). The dark seeds smell and taste sweet and slightly nutty; the white are lighter and more mellow in flavour. Toasting enhances the flavour. Poppy seeds are rich in protein and oil, but they go rancid quickly so buy small quantities.

Uses: Poppy seeds are mostly used in baking. In Europe and North America they go into breads, pretzels and cakes; Germany has *Mohntorte*, a poppy seed cake, and ground seeds mixed with honey are used to fill strudels. In Turkey roasted and ground seeds are made into halva; in India they are used to thicken kormas and curries. Use them to coat crusty vegetables and to dress noodles.

SAFFRON ● ●
Crocus sativus
The saffron crocus flowers in autumn. The flowers are picked by hand, the three thread-like stigmas removed and then toasted, releasing a heady, sensual aroma. This labour-intensive work is still done largely on family farms, and around 80,000 crocuses yield 2.5kg stigmas, which produce 500g of saffron. Always a commodity of great commercial value, saffron remains the most

expensive spice in the world. Fortunately, only a few threads of saffron are needed to give its musky warmth to a dish; too much will give a bitter flavour.

The crocus is native to western Asia. Persians, Phoenicians, Assyrians and Egyptians all used saffron as a dye, in beauty preparations, and in food and wine. Homer wrote of the "saffron-robed dawn" in the *Iliad*, and the *Song of Solomon* speaks of "saffron, sweet cane and cinnamon". Apicius gave recipes for fish with saffron and for saffron-flavoured wines. The Arabs took saffron to Spain in the 11th century, but it didn't reach northern Europe until the 14th century.

The best saffron has deep red, wiry threads; yellow threads indicate lesser quality. The aroma is rich, floral, honeyed and musky, the taste subtle yet penetrating, warm, earthy and lingering. The best quality comes from Iran, Kashmir and Spain and production is growing in other parts of the world.

Uses: Saffron is usually infused in liquid to release the aroma and colour before use. Its flavour is essential to many dishes, including Mediterranean fish soups, Catalan paella, Milanese risotto, Iranian polo and Mughal biryani. It is excellent with baked fish, chicken and rabbit. The Swedes make saffron buns for St Lucia's Day on 13 December, and saffron cake can still be found in England. Green tea infused with saffron is popular in Kashmir.

SESAME •
Sesamum indicum

Sesame has long been cultivated in Asia and Africa. High in polyunsaturated fatty acids, sesame oil is excellent for using in cooking. Excavations in Turkey show evidence of oil extracted from seeds in 900 BCE. The Babylonians and Egyptians used ground seeds in their breads, a practice still common in the Middle East. Sesame reached the Americas with African slaves.

Seeds are small, flat and waxy and may be white, golden, brown or black, depending on the variety. They are not aromatic, but have a mild, nutty flavour, drawn out by roasting.

Uses: Sesame is the main ingredient of Middle Eastern halva, and of Indian til ladoo. It is essential to the spice blends za'atar and shichimi-togarashi (p62). Black sesame is used in oriental cooking as a garnish for rice and vegetables. The Chinese enjoy the crunchy texture of sesame seeds coating foods such as prawn balls. The Japanese combine white seed with soy and sugar to dress noodles and salads. Dark, oriental sesame oil is made from dry roasted seeds and is used as a dressing. Sesame goes well with aubergines, courgettes, greens, noodles and rice, and it makes a good garnish for a range of beef stews.

SICHUAN PEPPER and SANSHO ● ●
Zanthoxylum simulans, Z piperitum

Both spices are the fruit of a prickly ash tree – one native to the Sichuan province of China, the other to Japan. Neither is related to the peppercorns of *Piper nigrum*.

Sichuan pepper is fragrant, warm and peppery with citrus notes. Sansho has a cleansing lemon-lime flavour. Both have a pleasantly numbing, tingling effect in the mouth.

Uses: Sichuan pepper is an ingredient in Chinese five-spice powder (p59), and combines well with ginger and star anise. It is particularly successful with poultry, pork, and squid or cuttlefish. The first step in using the split pods is often to roast them in a heavy, dry frying pan to release their aroma. Keep the heat low, shake the pan, and make sure they don't burn. Hua jiao yan, a blend of Sichuan pepper and salt, is used as a condiment for grilled or deep-fried foods. Sansho is ground and used as a table condiment, and in shichimi-togarashi (p62). It flavours miso soup, noodles and pickles and is most notably served with eel and grilled dishes that need zest. It also accompanies fried chicken, duck and egg dishes.

STAR ANISE ● ●
Illicium verum
This attractive spice, native to southern China and Vietnam, is now grown more widely in Asia. It has been cultivated for thousands of years for medicinal and culinary use. An irregular eight-pointed star, star anise is the fruit of an evergreen of the magnolia family. The aromatic, canoe-shaped carpels reveal glossy brown seeds. Star anise has a warm, sweet, anise-liquorice aroma; the flavour is sweetly pungent and slightly numbing, the aftertaste pleasantly fresh.

Uses: In China it is essential to five-spice powder (p59) and the soy sauce and spice blend used in the rich cooking liquor for red-cooked meats. Vietnamese braised dishes and pho (beef and noodle soup) are flavoured with star anise.

Star anise is still little used in western cookery, except

to flavour pastis and anisette, and in syrups and confectionery. It deserves to be better known; the sweet anise flavours combine well with root vegetables, squash and leeks, as well as seafood and beef. Try it with poached figs, pears or plums, and combine it with cinnamon, chilli, coriander or Sichuan pepper.

SUMAC ●
Rhus coriaria

The bushy sumac tree grows wild and is cultivated in Iran, Turkey and Sicily, and on other high plateaux of the Middle East. Its leaves turn red in autumn and the flowers develop into dense, conical clusters of deep crimson fruits. Picked just before fully ripe, they are dried in the sun and crushed to a brick red or red-brown coarse powder.

Uses: Lightly aromatic, fruity and tart, sumac is primarily a souring agent. Cracked berries can be soaked in water for 20 minutes, then pressed to extract the juice to use in dressings and marinades. The powder is rubbed on fish, kebabs and vegetables before cooking. It provides the tart flavour in Lebanese fattoush. A sprinkling of sumac will bring out the flavours in foods – try it on avocado or red onion. It goes well with yogurt and labneh, walnuts and pine nuts, and can be combined with coriander, cumin or mint. It is an essential ingredient in the spice mixture za'atar (p62).

TAMARIND
Tamarindus indica
Indigenous to eastern Africa, the tamarind tree is familiar throughout the tropics and sub-tropics. The tall, handsome trees, valued for their food, medicine and wood products, remain productive for up to 200 years. Well known in the Middle East before medieval times, in England during Tudor times tamarind was appreciated for its thirst-quenching properties.

The curved fruit pods turn dark brown as they ripen. They contain a brown, sticky, acidic pulp and black seeds. The brittle shells are removed and the pulp is pressed into flat cakes or further processed into pastes or concentrates. Tamarind has little smell, and a pleasant, faintly fruity, tingling acidic taste. The sour notes come from its high tartaric acid content, which makes it an excellent souring agent.

Uses: In India and Southeast Asia tamarind is the main acidulant in spiced lentil dishes, chutneys and sherbets. It provides the sour note in Goan vindaloo. In Indonesia, where the word *asem* means both tamarind and sour, it gives beef rendang its tang. Its flavour can be detected in Thai tom yam soup and nahm prik. In Costa Rica it makes a sour sauce, and carbonated tamarind drinks are popular throughout the Caribbean and in Mexico. It is also an ingredient of Worcestershire Sauce.

TURMERIC ● ●
Curcuma longa

This member of the ginger family is valued throughout southern Asia for its musky, sharp flavour, its vibrant colour, as a medicine and for use in rituals. India is the biggest producer and consumer.

The rhizomes, also called fingers, may be sold fresh, or are boiled briefly to arrest maturation, then sun-dried for around two weeks until very hard. The fingers are polished and crushed to produce the vivid orange powder. Turmeric powder will retain its colour indefinitely, but its earthy flavour with citrus overtones will disappear over time.

Uses: In some foods, such as mustard and piccalilli, turmeric is used for its colour rather than its taste. It combines well with other spices and forms the basis of many masalas and curry pastes. It goes into Indian

fish, meat, egg and vegetable dishes, Indonesian rendang and Moroccan chermoula. Use turmeric with rice, pulses and root vegetables.
Fresh turmeric is lightly aromatic, with notes of orange and ginger, and a slightly bitter aftertaste. It is used in spice pastes with lemongrass, shallots and chillies; it is grated into stews and laksas and its juice flavours rice dishes. Try it with poultry and fish; combine with chillies, coriander, cumin, coconut milk, ginger or lemongrass.

VANILLA ● ●
Vanilla planifolia
The fruit of an orchid native to Central America, vanilla was prized by the Aztecs. A subject tribe had learnt to ferment the bean-like fruits to extract vanillin crystals. Moctezuma offered a chocolate drink flavoured with vanilla to Cortés, who took both to Spain, where it was named *vainilla*, meaning "little pod". By the second half of the 16th century the vanilla chocolate drink had conquered Europe.

Vanilla is expensive to produce; unripe beans are harvested and subjected to a complicated curing process. They oxidise, turn black and sometimes have a light dusting of *givre* (white crystals).

The pods develop a rich, mellow, floral aroma and sweetly fruity or creamy flavour. It takes around 10kg fresh pods to yield 1kg of vanilla. The high cost led scientists to produce synthetic vanillin in 1874; inferior to real vanilla, it is still used in many commercial products. If buying vanilla extract, check it is "natural vanilla extract".

Uses: Vanilla is mostly used in sweet foods, including ice cream, syrups and fruits. A single pod will flavour a jar of sugar. It enhances the flavour of chocolate, coffee, cinnamon, cardamom and wattleseed. Vanilla-flavoured savoury dishes, including seafood, poultry and root vegetables, are becoming increasingly popular.

WASABI •
Eutrema wasabi

Sometimes classified as a spice, other times as a herb, wasabi is related to horseradish and mustard. A perennial plant, native to the cold mountain streams of Japan, the crop is limited, and cultivation is now established in New Zealand, California and the UK. Wasabi is very expensive to produce; it can only be cultivated in pure, cold running water.

Wasabi is sometimes called Japanese horseradish because of its pungency, and also because, like horseradish, the rhizome is the edible part. This intense and sharp pungency assails the nose first; the taste is biting yet fresh and cleansing.

The rhizome is peeled and grated finely and served in a small mound, or made into a paste.

Fresh wasabi is seldom found outside Japan. Tubes of paste or tins of powder are also available. In the West, many "wasabi" pastes are in fact made with horseradish coloured green.
USES: Wasabi is the classic accompaniment to sushi or sashimi, to be blended to individual taste with soy sauce. Many chefs put a fine layer of wasabi between the fish and vinegared rice in their sushi. A small amount of wasabi will also give a piquant note to dressings and marinades.

WATTLESEED •
Acacia species
Only a few of the acacias growing in the Australian outback are edible; *A aneura* and *A victoria* are those usually harvested for wattleseed. Indigenous people have long used the bark and roots

medicinally, and the highly nutritious green seeds are a mainstay of the diet. Roasted and ground seeds are transformed into a rich, brown powder resembling coffee. This is the spice that became popular in the late 20th century.

Wattleseed is expensive because of the multiple processes involved in its production. There are now some plantations in existence, but much is still gathered from the wild.

Uses: The toasty, raisin, chocolate and hazelnut aromatics make it a perfect spice for ice cream, custard, mousse and yogurt. It is good in pancakes, biscuits and breads, and wattle liquid can be brewed in a coffeemaker to use in smoothies or to drink as an alternative to coffee. Combine wattleseed with thyme, mace or coriander, and pepper as a rub for chicken, beef, lamb and kangaroo.

SPICES OF THE WORLD

4. Spice mixtures

There are dozens of spice mixtures, powders, pastes and seasonings in existence, some specific to a particular country or region, some to a specific dish. Here are some popular spice blends and their key ingredients

Advieh This is a Persian blend for rice containing cinnamon, dried rose petals, cumin and cardamom.

Baharat The Arabic word for spice, this blend from the Middle East varies from country to country. It gives depth to pulses, grains, sauces and soups, and is rubbed onto fish and meat. Basic ingredients are pepper, coriander, cardamom, cumin, cassia or cinnamon, and nutmeg.

Barbecue A blend of pepper, cumin, cayenne, paprika, thyme, salt and sugar used as a dry rub.

Cajun Cajun seasoning flavours the blackened fish and chicken, and the gumbos and jambalayas of Louisiana. It contains paprika, pepper, cayenne, fennel, cumin, thyme, oregano, garlic and salt.

Chinese five-spice powder A blend of star anise, fennel, cassia, Sichuan pepper and cloves. Use sparingly in slow-cooked dishes, to season meat or poultry and stir-fried vegetables.

Curry powder Typically contains cumin, coriander, pepper, ginger, turmeric, fenugreek and chilli. Whole spices are dry roasted before being ground. Other spices may be added and the proportions of spices varies.

Dukka This Egyptian nut and spice blend combines hazelnuts, sesame, coriander, cumin, nigella and salt. It can be served as a snack or sprinkled over salads, vegetables and labneh.

Garam masala Ingredients vary from region to region in India, but it typically contains cardamom, cinnamon, cumin, pepper, cloves and coriander. It is usually added towards the end of cooking to preserve aromas.

Harissa Made from chillies, caraway, coriander, cumin, garlic, sweet red pepper, salt and olive oil, this north African paste is used in tagines and stews and as an accompaniment to kebabs, couscous and breads.

Jamaican jerk seasoning A combination of allspice, pepper, chilli, nutmeg, cinnamon and thyme. Use it as a rub for meats to be barbecued.

Khmeli-suneli This Georgian mix of coriander, fenugreek, fennel, dried marigold, mint, dill, savory and cloves can be rubbed onto meats or used in vegetable dishes and soups.

Panch phoron Contains cumin, fennel, mustard, nigella and fenugreek. Use to flavour pulses and vegetables.

Quâlat daqqa A Tunisian blend for lamb, vegetables and chickpeas, made from pepper, cloves, grains of paradise, cinnamon and nutmeg.

Quatre-épices A mix of pepper, nutmeg, cloves and ginger. Use in casseroles and braised dishes, as well as to flavour pork and hams. It flavours gingerbread and pain d'épices, and is widely used in charcuterie.

Ras el hanout A Moroccan mixture of 20 or more spices. Allspice, anise, cardamom, cassia, cloves, fennel, ginger, grains of paradise, mace, nutmeg, pepper, dried rosebuds, saffron and turmeric are among the ingredients; some versions are floral, others pungent. Use sparingly in tagines, with lamb and in rice.

Recado rojo A south Mexican paste containing annatto, coriander, pepper, cumin, cloves, garlic, oregano, salt and bitter orange juice. It's essential to meat or fish to be baked or steamed, and flavours empanadas and tamales.

Sambar powder A south Indian blend of coriander, cumin, pepper, mustard, fenugreek, chilli, turmeric and asafoetida, often used with pulses and vegetables.

Shichimi-togarashi A combination of black and white sesame, sansho, poppy seed, chilli, dried tangerine peel and nori flakes. Use as a condiment with tempura or noodles, and rub on fish or meat before grilling or frying. Also known as seven-spice mixture.

Za'atar Containing sesame, sumac, and dried za'atar or thyme, this Middle Eastern blend is widely used to sprinkle on meatballs, kebabs and vegetables.

5. Matching spicy food and wine

What to look for when choosing wines to accompany a range of popular spicy dishes

Not being an enthusiastic beer drinker, I have long experimented with wines to accompany spicy food.

What is often needed is a cool wine with refreshing acidity to counteract the heat in the food. Spicy flavours come in many different forms, from the chilli hit of some Thai, Indonesian or Mexican dishes, or the hot, salty, sweet-sour flavours of Vietnam, to the more subtle flavours of korma, biryani or a Hungarian goulash. It would be very difficult, and unwise, to assert that a certain wine would or would not go well with a particular spice or blend because much depends on the amount of spice and the main ingredients in the dish.

However, there are three elements that are best avoided when selecting a wine to accompany most spicy food – high alcohol, oakiness and high tannins.

Alcohol levels
Highly spiced food has many complex flavours and tends to clash with high alcohol levels in a wine. Chilli, in particular, increases awareness of alcohol, so it is best to choose wines with medium or low abv. Zesty, aromatic wines with a hint of residual sugar help reduce the chilli effect without diminishing appreciation of the spices.

Oak influence
Oak imparts tannin and some spice notes to wine and is best avoided, or at least kept to a minimum. Heavily oaked wines are likely to clash with the spices in the dish and both will be spoiled.

Tannins
Spices tend to emphasise tannins in wine and may give the wine a bitter note. Avoid firm, drying tannins; choose a fruity, mellow red wine with silky tannins.

Keep the ambient temperature in mind, too; in hot climates, full-bodied wines do not drink well. Rich, full-bodied wines, both white and red, can often be disappointing in a hot environment.

Ideally the texture and intensity of the food and wine should be matched, and the wine should be fruit-led. It isn't easy to achieve a perfect pairing where both wine and dish complement each other if you haven't made the dish yourself and know its spice profile, or discussed it with the chef, but the suggestions to follow may help. These wines generally work well with a range of spicy foods, although with the considerable variations in spiced dishes from different parts of the world – and the differences in wines – this is by no means an exhaustive list and I suggest readers experiment with their own spicy food and wine pairings.

Thai red, green and massaman curries, hot Malay and Indian curries such as Madras, jalfrezi or vindaloo, Mexican pibil
Fresh white wines with crisp acidity, low or medium alcohol levels and a hint of sweetness such as Pinot Gris, Riesling Kabinett or Spätlese, or Grüner Veltliner pair well with highly spiced dishes, or try a full-bodied rosé. Gewürztraminer can be a good match, but sometimes the rose notes can be too dominant or the wine may be too sweet. If you have a meat curry and prefer a red wine,

chose a lighter style with soft tannins such as Tempranillo, Gamay, cool-climate Shiraz or Merlot.

Tandoori chicken, lamb kebab
A supple, fruity red would be a good choice – try Merlot, Pinot Noir, Gamay or Zinfandel.

Milder Indian dishes such as korma, pasanda, biryani
For these dishes, whether made with chicken, fish or vegetables, the broader flavours of unoaked Chardonnay, Semillon or Viognier work well.

Dahls, vegetable dishes with paneer or yogurt
Fuller, rounded white wines can go well with these creamy dishes. Try a Semillon, Marsanne, Pinot Gris or a creamy Chardonnay.

Thai stir-fried dishes
The umami elements – oyster sauce, soy, garlic and ginger – in these dishes benefit from fruity, supple red wines such as Pinot Noir, Gamay or Zweigelt. For whites, opt for a Pinot Blanc or unoaked Chardonnay.

Peking duck
Pinot Gris is a good match for the smokiness of the duck, or try a Riesling Spätlese, an Albariño, or a Beaujolais cru.

Sichuan dishes
With spicy dishes such as Mapo tofu and pork, or garlicky, spiced noodles, the honeyed acidity of Chenin Blanc or the spicy acidity of Grüner Veltliner are particularly complementary. Sicilian Grillo

is also worth considering, as is a Beaujolais cru or a light Pinot Noir. Pork belly with garlic and chilli oil needs a wine to cut through the richness. Try a Malbec, or a cool-climate Shiraz or Grenache. Dandan noodles are well matched with a medium-weight rosé and even with Champagne. Avoid wines with sweet fruit because they do not marry well with the combination of oil and spice in much Sichuan food.

Chinese spiced prawns, sesame chicken, dim sum, Vietnamese salads and spring rolls
The floral notes of Viognier or a grassy Semillon go well with the citrus and ginger flavours of many of these dishes. Riesling Kabinett and Grüner Veltliner are other good choices.

Sushi, sashimi, tempura
Saké would be the local choice. Champagne, fino sherry, Grüner Veltliner, Albariño, Riesling Kabinett or a Provençal rosé would also match these foods.

Moroccan tagines
In north Africa tagines are usually served with a local rosé. Try a Lebanese or southern French rosé or a mellow red wine such as Syrah, Rioja or Grenache.

Middle Eastern and Indian kebabs/Indonesian satays
A supple red wine is the best choice for these meaty dishes. Syrah, Grenache, Tempranillo or Merlot would be a fitting accompaniment.

Vietnamese and Mexican dishes with coriander, citrus flavours
Aromatic white wines such as Albariño, Pinot Gris or Sauvignon Blanc support these flavours well. Or you could try a light red such as a Beaujolais cru or a Cabernet Franc.

Tomato and tomatillo-based dishes
Many Tex-Mex and Mexican dishes have an acidic tomato element alongside the chilli. Few red wines marry well with the acidity, so it is best to look for a white – try a crisp Albariño, Sauvignon Blanc, Godello or Pinot Grigio, or a light rosé.

Where to buy spices

Buy your spices from a reputable spice merchant. You may have a good local supplier, particularly if you live in Asia, but if not, try one of these online specialist spice merchants:

Australia
- Herbie's Spices; www.herbies.com.au

Canada
- The Silk Road Spice Merchant; www.thespicetrade.ca

France
- Epices Roellinger; www.epices-roellinger.com
- Thiercelin 1809; www.thiercelin.com

Germany
- Schuhbeck; www.schuhbeck.de

Hong Kong and Taiwan
- Regency Spices; www.regencyspices.hk

India
- Catch; www.catchfoods.com
- MDH; www.mdhspices.com

Japan
- Ambika Trading Company; www.ambikajapan.com

Malaysia
- Baba's; www.babas.com.my

UK
- Seasoned Pioneers; www.seasonedpioneers.com
- Spice Mountain; www.spicemountain.co.uk
- Steenbergs Spices; www.steenbergs.co.uk

USA
- Kalustyans; www.kalustyans.com
- Penzeys Spices; www.penzeys.com

Bibliography

Collingham, Lizzie, *Curry*, Vintage, 2006

David, Elizabeth, *Spices, Salt and Aromatics in the English Kitchen*, Penguin, 1970

Dalby, Andrew, *Dangerous Tastes*, British Museum Press, 2000

Freedman, Paul, *Out of the East*, Yale University Press, 2008

Hemphill, Ian, *The Spice and Herb Bible*, Robert Rose, 2006

Hildebrand, Caz, *The Grammar of Spice*, Thames & Hudson, 2017

Keay, John, *The Spice Route: A History*, John Murray, 2005

McGee, Harold, *On Food and Cooking*, Hodder & Stoughton, 2004

Merrett, Paul, *Spice Odyssey*, Kyle Books, 2013

Nabhan, Gary Paul, *Cumin, Camels and Caravans: A Spice Odyssey*, University of California Press, 2014

Norman, Jill, *Herbs and Spices, The Cook's Reference*, Dorling Kindersley, 2015

Parle, Stevie and Grazette, Emma, *Spice Trip*, Square Peg, 2012